The Law of Attraction and Your Financial Situation

The Law of Attraction and Your Financial Situation

Table Of Contents

Chapter 1:
   The *Law of Attraction* – What It Really Is and What It Is Not

Chapter 2:
   Objective and Subjective Thinking

Chapter 3:
   Stop the Default Processes from Ruling Your Life

Chapter 4:
   Pivoting Your Thought Process

Chapter 5:
   The Right Mindset about Money

Chapter 6:
   Wealth Manifestation through the *Law of Attraction*

Chapter 7:
   Is a Poor Person Who Thinks Positively about Money Rich?

Chapter 8:
   What about Lotteries and Windfall Incomes?

Chapter 9:
   Balancing the Inner Self and the Outer Self

Chapter 10:
   Why Doesn't Everyone that Uses the *Law of Attraction* Become Rich?

Introduction

With the release of The Secret followed by the outstanding response it has garnered, a lot of people are speaking about the Law of Attraction. The problem is that not half of these people know what they are talking about.

The Law of Attraction is not an enchantment or a potion that will wish all your problems away. There are things that need to be done if you want to experience its richness in your life.

This eBook specifically deals with the implementation of the Law of Attraction in gathering money, but really it is about all its various applications that can help in improving your life.

Sit back, free up your mind from all its clutter, and have a good read.

Chapter 1:

The *Law of Attraction* – What It Really Is and What It Is Not

Chapter 2:

Objective and Subjective Thinking

- → We must begin a thought process for it, and begin vociferously asking the universe to make it happen.
- → We must then visualize a situation wherein we already have what we are hankering for, and we must live in that reality.
- → At the same time, we must not attach ourselves to what might happen. We must only think about having it. There is no room for apprehension.

In this eBook, we are going to expose various aspects of the *Law of Attraction* and see how we can apply it in one of the most important areas of our lives – attracting money. Can one really become rich by just thinking vividly about it? We need to understand the law better and learn how to implement it in order to get these answers.

The *Law of Attraction* – What It Really Is and What It Is Not

It is somewhat amazing to see how much talk there is about the *Law of Attraction* and how few people actually know about what it is. The *Law of Attraction* is not a spell that you use and things begin happening that way. It is not that you chant 'like begets like' a thousand times a day and see things happening the way you want. If the *Law of Attraction* were so simple, we would have already witnessed the world as a much better place by now.

People explain the *Law of Attraction* in various ways. The commonest definition you will find will be something like this:-
"If you strongly believe that something should happen, it will certainly happen."

A sentence couldn't be any simpler, but you will immediately realize that this raises more questions than it answers. The question of desires is the most important. Is it only what we desire *and* think about strongly that will happen? Or will things that we don't desire also happen if we somehow think strongly about them? Then there is also the question of internal conflict of thoughts. At times, there could be situations where we think equally in both ways. For example, we may think that a job could be ours or not. So how do we apply the *Law of Attraction* in such a case? Or what do we do when we are thinking strongly about something and someone else is thinking strongly about the exact opposite thing? What will happen in that case?

In order to be able to reply all these questions, it is important to first understand what the *Law of Attraction* really says.

Notwithstanding the various ways in which the *Law of Attraction* has been defined, we can break things down in the following four elements:-
  → We must know <u>*exactly*</u> what we want.

Summary

Let us begin by understanding what the Law of Attraction really is all about.

Summary

Since the Law of Attraction is so strongly based in the thought process, we must first learn what our thought processes really are.

Objective and Subjective Thinking

One of the main steps toward understanding the *Law of Attraction* to a greater degree is to understand what the word 'thought' really means. Throughout the description of this law, you will find that it doesn't refer to thinking in the way that we do. We think that we exist, we are in a particular situation, there are certain people with and around us, there are things we are with and so on. Whatever we see becomes real for us, and that becomes a part of our thought. However, this is not the kind of thought process that the *Law of Attraction* talks about. This is known as objective thinking.

But, in order to see the implementation of the *Law of Attraction* in our lives, we have to first shun the concept of objective thinking. We have to adopt a higher level of thinking, which is subjective thinking.

Why do we think that our spouse is real? Because we can see them. But this is objective thinking.

With subjective thinking, things will be the other way round. *We think our spouse is real and therefore we see them.* Now, that is subjective thinking.

Your job isn't real. But because you believe so concretely that it is real, it becomes a reality for you.

Your situations aren't real. However, your firm belief that they are happening makes them real for you.

This is the realm of subjective thinking. When you think subjectively, things are more or less like how you are seeing a dream. When we see a dream, how do we picture ourselves? Is our 'dream' self the real us? No, we are the ones who are 'seeing' the dream. We are just the frame of reference, the consciousness.

Whatever is happening in our dream is our perspective. That is how thinking works in the subjective world.

In this world, what we see is actually just a manifestation of our thoughts. Now, that doesn't mean those things aren't real. What that means is that those things are present in our consciousness. Just as we might be able to alter things in our dreams, by applying the *Law of Attraction*, we could alter things in our 'real' life as well.

Chapter 3:

Stop the Default Processes from Ruling Your Life

Summary

We give a lot of focus to things that are irrelevant in our lives, so much so that they actually start ruling our existence. But there are ways in which we can stop them from toying with us.

Stop the Default Processes from Ruling Your Life

To a large extent, we allow things and situations to rule over us. How many times in life do we tell, "This situation is beyond me! I cannot do anything about it."? We do that a lot. Each time that we do that, we are yielding the control of our lives to the situations that are governing us. We do not think even one bit in the way that the *Law of Attraction* suggests us to do.

And what is that way?

Quite simply put, that way is to think as though <u>we</u> rule the circumstances. The fact is that these circumstances are much in our hands. It is up to us to create situations that are conducive for our development, and not the other way round.

Think about it. Is a financial problem bogging you down? Probably you have planned an endeavor but aren't able to do so because of paucity of funds. So what do you do? Most people will think that this going nowhere and they will bail themselves out. But a person who really believes subjectively will understand that the financial problem lies in the frame of reference and will not worry about it too much. On the other hand, such a person will try to think that he or she <u>could make</u> the situation conducive.

Sounds impractical? It isn't so impractical actually. If you begin to think strongly about having money, what will you do? The *Law of Attraction* tells you that you have to 'visualize' it and actually behave as though you have the money. In that case, you will apply for a loan probably and when you do that, you will be very confident because you *believe* that the money will be yours. Your confidence will work to your advantage because your potential financiers will get the impression that you have the capability to earn and pay them back. They understand you are a person of merit.

This is what the believers in the *Law of Attraction* do. They make things conducive to them through an intense thought process. But their thought process is not of this objective world. They think as though they are the center of everything that's happening and that they can have full control over the situations they face.

Chapter 4:

Pivoting Your Thought Process

Summary

So how do you go about developing this kind of thought process, where you think you are the center of the universe and everything just exists in your frame of reference?

Pivoting Your Thought Process

In order to create the subjective thought process that the *Law of Attraction* demands of you, it is very important that you create the right frame of reference. You have to be like the person seeing everything in a dream. Your perceived reality is actually the things that are happening in your frame of reference, which is just another name for your consciousness. But, you need to put a finger on this consciousness. You need to anchor it. This aspect – anchoring your conscious mind – is known as pivoting your thought process.

When you begin pivoting your thought process, the primary requirement is to have a fixed point from where you can begin. Usually, this fixed point is your resolve, your intention, your motive, your purpose. For example, if you really need to start a business, your resolution to do that is your pivot. The stronger you resolve to achieve that, the more profound your pivot will be. That is why people who have stronger resolutions are able to achieve better things than people who don't have a very strong mindset to achieve something.

If you consider your desire as your pivot and see everything from that perspective, everything begins falling into place. You feel as though everything that's happening is happening as a means of bringing you closer to your desire. In the above instance, if your desire to start a business is your pivot, then you feel as though everything happening in your life is taking you one step closer toward realizing your dreams. This includes the positives as well as negatives. If you suddenly meet someone, you feel that somehow that will be connected with your new business, which isn't yet started but you have no apprehensions in your mind about it. You also feel that your getting fired from your desk job was something that will take you closer to having your own business.

People who believe in the *Law of Attraction* staunchly build such pivots in their minds. Then on, their entire life is focused on this pivot. This is what drives them and motivates them into coming closer to their goals.

Chapter 5:

The Right Mindset about Money

Summary

We are applying the Law of Attraction to wealth. What is important here is the mindset that we need to make this application.

The Right Mindset about Money

What does the *Law of Attraction* tell us about money?

It is actually very important to point out that the *Law of Attraction* is not just about money. It is a very general law which can be applied to every aspect of our lives. This is a law that helps to enrich ourselves as people, not just financial entities. However, we are endeavoring to see how we can apply the *Law of Attraction* as regards attracting money.

That is the reason it becomes vital to know what kind of mindset you must have. If we try to implement the *Law of Attraction* to this concept, we must realize that a person who is actually trying to attract money should think about it all the time. Since thoughts attract results, this is what must happen.

However, the thoughts mustn't be objective. What are objective thoughts? Now, if you are only thinking about how many dollars you will earn on a particular project, then that is objective thinking. If you cannot think beyond numbers, all you are doing is thinking objectively. You are thinking how much you could make, how much you could save, etc. These are objective thoughts and, if you were to apply the *Law of Attraction*, you would understand that these thoughts won't attract the money to you.

Hence, you need to think subjectively. Don't think about the money itself, but think about <u>*what you must do*</u> in order to bring the money to you. Thinking about the quality of your product, for example, is a beautiful step in this regard. When you do that, you are actually improving the sales potential of your product and hence you are bringing in the money.

A person who believes in the *Law of Attraction* won't think – "I must sell this product because I want to earn money." Instead, such a person would think – "I must be honest in making this product and give it great quality so that I earn money out of it."

A person believing in the *Law of Attraction* automatically becomes honest because he or she knows what it takes to bring in the money. They don't believe in quick-fix solutions but always go for the long haul. This should be your mindset about money too – Don't think about how to actually bring in the money; think about what you must do in order to let the money come to you.

Chapter 6:

Wealth Manifestation through the *Law of Attraction*

Summary

The five steps you need in order to manifest wealth applying the Law.

Wealth Manifestation through the *Law of Attraction*

Here are the five things you need to do in order to manifest the wealth that you are expecting through the *Law of Attraction*.

Believe

The first step is to ingrain the thought of wealth in your subconscious. You have to think staunchly that you will be able to attain the large amount of wealth that you are hoping for.

Visualize

It is very important to actually visualize the wealth. You have to think that the wealth is already in your bank account and now what you will do with it. Begin thinking as if you are planning what to do with the money. You don't have it already, but that's not the point. The *Law of Attraction* tells that you have to be strong in your belief, and visualization is the best way to do that.

Be Grateful

Taking your belief one step forward, you must actually start thanking the universe for granting the wealth to you. Well, it has not already granted you the wealth, but you have no aspersions at all about that happening. You are darned sure that you will get the wealth and so being grateful is the next logical thing.

Listen to Your Heart

Your heart will tell you a lot of things at this point. It will tell you to do particular things. Do not stifle any of these "voices". Listen to them intently. Act upon them.

You have to make sure that you listen to every voice because any of them could be the one voice that opens the doors of opportunity to you.

Continue Your Actions

Never give up, never relent. Remember that stopping is a sign of weakness. You don't want the universe to understand that your belief is faltering. You want it to know that you will keep up no matter what. Sooner or later, your supreme confidence is going to bring the wealth at your door.

Chapter 7:

Is a Poor Person Who Thinks Positively about Money Rich?

Summary

Does only thought matter? If beggars think about horses, can they ride?

Is a Poor Person Who Thinks Positively about Money Rich?

This is a question that irks most people, especially those who hear about the *Law of Attraction* for the first time. After all, they think, the *Law of Attraction* speaks about thoughts begetting results, so if they were to think strongly about something, shouldn't they get that realized? In other words, if someone doesn't have a car and thinks strongly about it, they should be owners of the car, right?

Though that does sound very romantic, the problem is that the *Law of Attraction* does not work in that fashion. It is not about think-think-get-get. There are a lot of under layers here. Firstly, people who think about the *Law of Attraction* in this manner don't bring a very important thing into the equation – the emphasis of effort. You don't get much without channelizing your thoughts into action.

Let us understand this better with an example. Suppose you have an ambition to open a restaurant. Right now, it's just your ambition. Yes, you are thinking so strongly about it that you can taste it, but that's just about it. Will that make your restaurant then?

The answer is quite obvious – No. The *Law of Attraction* is not about sitting on your bean bag watching a DVD and expecting your inner desires to manifest themselves. You have to actually let the thought out of your system. You have to let it come out and become action.

When you think strongly about something, there will be an inner voice that will tell you to act in a particular way. If you are looking at opening a restaurant, a small voice within you will tell you to start hunting for good places. The voice will tell you to learn the art of hotel management. The voice will also tell you to begin gathering funds. There are so many things that will be spoken by this still small voice. The important thing is that you have to listen to it. And you have to act upon it.

It is only when you begin translating these thoughts into actions will you be able to do something about realizing them.

So a beggar who merely thinks about a horse won't be able to do something soon. However, if he thinks how he should get the horse and start implementing those ideas, there is all likelihood that he will be atop one soon enough.

Chapter 8:

What about Lotteries and Windfall Incomes?

Summary

What does the Law of Attraction have to say about lotteries and all other kinds of overnight richness modes?

What about Lotteries and Windfall Incomes?

A very commonly asked question by most people is whether they can win lotteries and have other kinds of lucky breaks merely by having a strong belief in them, just as the *Law of Attraction* would have them do. They think very strongly about winning and so why should they not win? They even think about winning all the time, they buy tickets by the dozen, so the winners should be them, right?

The problem is that these people are in the right premise, but they aren't implementing it in the right way. So, what's the right way? Can you use the *Law of Attraction* to win a lottery?

Well, for that, the first thing is to think rightly about it. You must not expect a spell to come into action bringing gold coins at your door. This won't happen. But you could align things to work your way. Think positively about winning. When you do that, things automatically begin happening in a way that's beneficial to you. You probably won't become a millionaire overnight, but maybe your strong beliefs will help you win small amounts and be happy about them.

But there are ways in which you can go against the *Law of Attraction* here. If you expect too much, it's wrong. The *Law of Attraction* tells you to have a strong belief, but it does not tell you to expect a particular kind of result. Simply visualize what would happen if you are a winner of a particular sum, however, don't force the universe into granting you that sum. In the same vein, if you start getting grumpy if you are not making the kind of income you think you should, you are undoing all your positive belief. Grumpiness is a sign of disbelief and hence it is a sign of weakness.

People who win lotteries think somehow that they deserved the victory. If you were to ask them, they will say that they visualized winning the lottery at some point in their lives and they imagined it so vividly that they felt it was for real.

Try that. Imagine. Visualize your result. Don't go overboard. Don't over-expect. Things will begin aligning your way. But be ready to accept, without grudging, whatever comes your way. It will be better than what you have, if your belief is in the right.

Chapter 9:

Balancing the Inner Self and the Outer Self

Summary

If you really follow the Law of Attraction, you have to work at striking the right balance between your inner and outer selves.

Balancing the Inner Self and the Outer Self

One of the most significant applications of the *Law of Attraction* is to balance our inner and outer selves. Our inner self is our consciousness. It is the way we think and behave. This is where the *Law of Attraction* begins to take effect. The *Law of Attraction* starts manifesting itself when we think and that begins in our inner self. Our outer self is characterized by our action. The way we act and implement our thought processes is how our outer self functions.

If we have to make the best utilization of the *Law of Attraction* into our life, then it is essential that we learn how to create the balance between our inner and outer selves. It is vital that we put into action what we think. What begins as a thought manifestation must get converted into action.

If you were to just think and sit about getting a new house, it isn't going to happen. Yes, if your thoughts are strong, if your belief is strong, the universe will begin aligning itself toward making things happen. But now, it is you who has to act. If you don't even lift a finger things aren't going to happen. Now, you have to put your outer self into action. This is when the positive energies that have been created start taking shape and things begin happening.

The problem with most of us is that we use our inner self to think and believe. We say so often that we want to do a particular thing but only a few of us actually put our outer selves into action mode.

The *Law of Attraction* will make things happen. But it will restrict itself to aligning things in a particular way. The rest is your call. It will make you confident about doing certain things, and that is what will influence the people around you and things will happen positively for you, but the main thing for that to happen is that you have to take the initiative and act.

Chapter 10:
Why Doesn't Everyone that Uses the *Law of Attraction* Become Rich?

Summary

A lot of people might think about the Law of Attraction. But only a few of them actually begin climbing the steps of success and really become rich.

Why Doesn't Everyone that Uses the *Law of Attraction* Become Rich?

If you have been following through so far, you will have realized two things:-
- → The *Law of Attraction* is a definite reality; everyone puts it to use.
- → However, a lot of people don't really put it to use the right way.

There is no refuting the strength of the *Law of Attraction* in channelizing the energies of the universe in such a way that things can begin to happen favorably. But the problem is that, the *Law of Attraction* will only channelize these things. If we don't make use of the energies to achieve what we are hankering after, it's all going to be a lost cause.

For example, if you only think about becoming rich but don't do anything actively in that regard, there's no way that you will become rich. In fact, even if you win through a lottery, you have to make the effort of buying the lottery and tracking the winnings.

The bottom line is clear – the *Law of Attraction* works but only if you put it to use. These are the things that you must do sequentially:-
- → You must strongly believe that a particular thing will happen. Your belief should be strong and unwavering, so unshakable that nothing must twist your belief in any way.
- → Then you have to visualize this thing, as though it has actually happened with you and that you are enjoying its fruits.
- → The next step will be to begin acting upon your inner voice. You will hear your inner voice a lot when you strongly believe in something. Acting upon this is what will bring you closer to realizing your ambitions.

So, if you are planning on becoming rich through the *Law of Attraction*, the important thing for you is to believe and then act. Without either of them, nothing is going to fall into place.

Conclusion

The Law of Attraction can make you rich. You must have heard it a lot. Now you know what it takes to get there.

All the best to you!!!

www.ingramcontent.com/pod-product-compliance
Lightning Source LLC
LaVergne TN
LVHW012131070526
838202LV00056B/5948